THANK YOU FOR PURCHASING TEA &
COFFEE OCEAN TREASURES. IF YOU
ENJOYED YOUR COLORING EXPERIENCE,
PLEASE CHECK OUT THESE OTHER BOOKS
BY ME AT AMAZON.COM:

VINTAGE WINE GARDEN

VINTAGE PARIS BAKE SHOP

ICE CREAM MADNESS

TEA & COFFEE TROPICAL TREASURES

TEA & COFFEE TREASURES

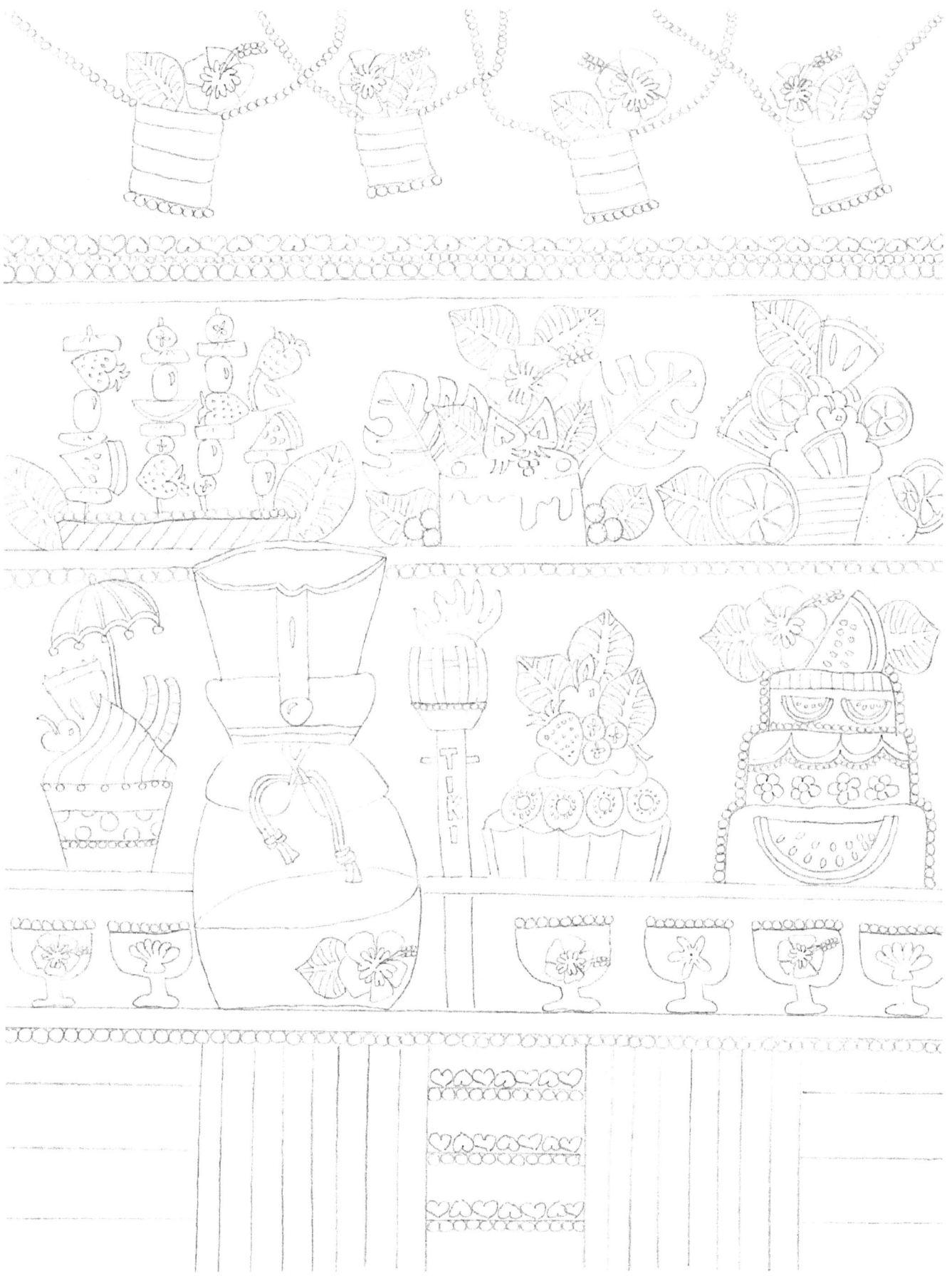

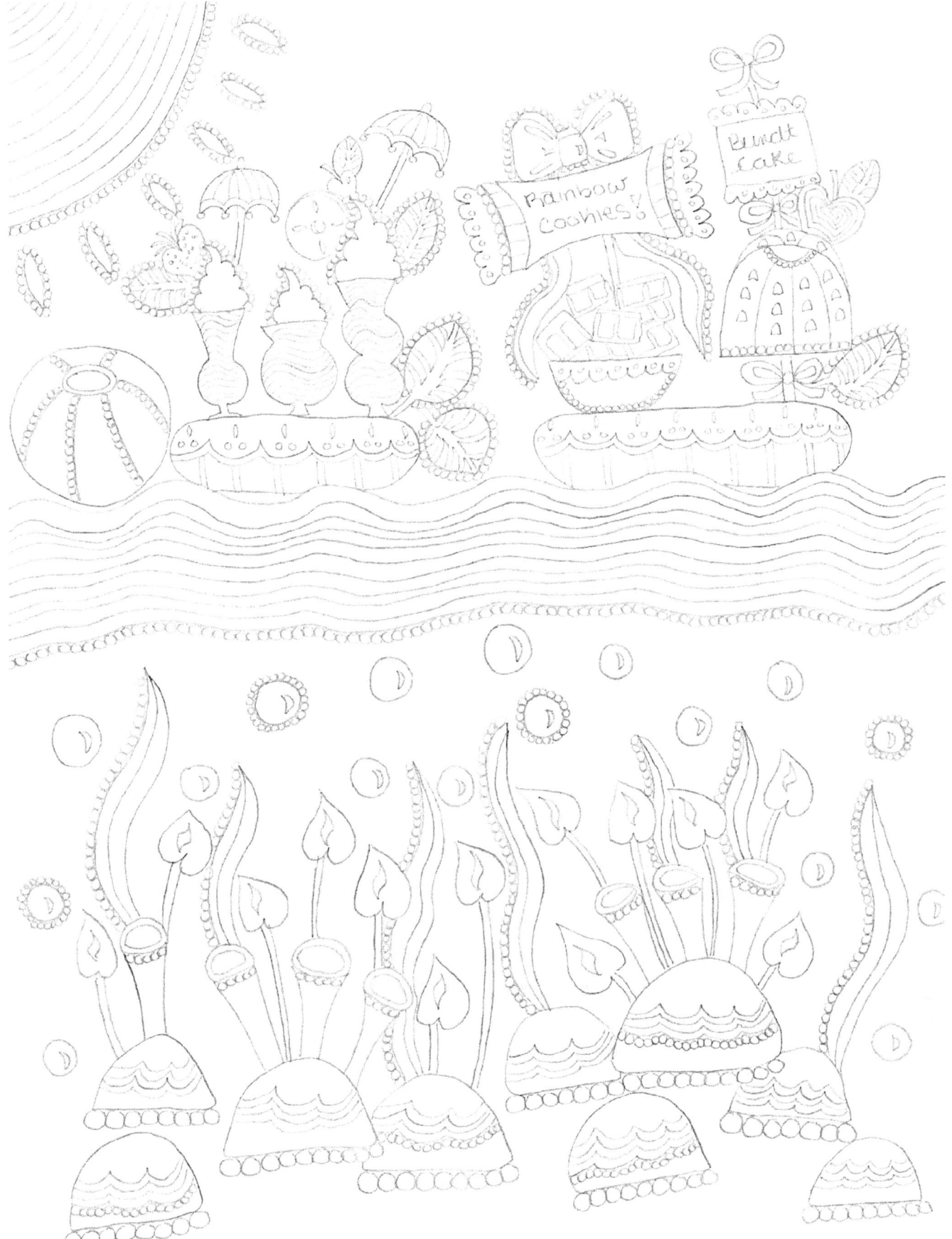

iced strawberry coffee

iced banana chai coffee

iced cherry matcha coffee

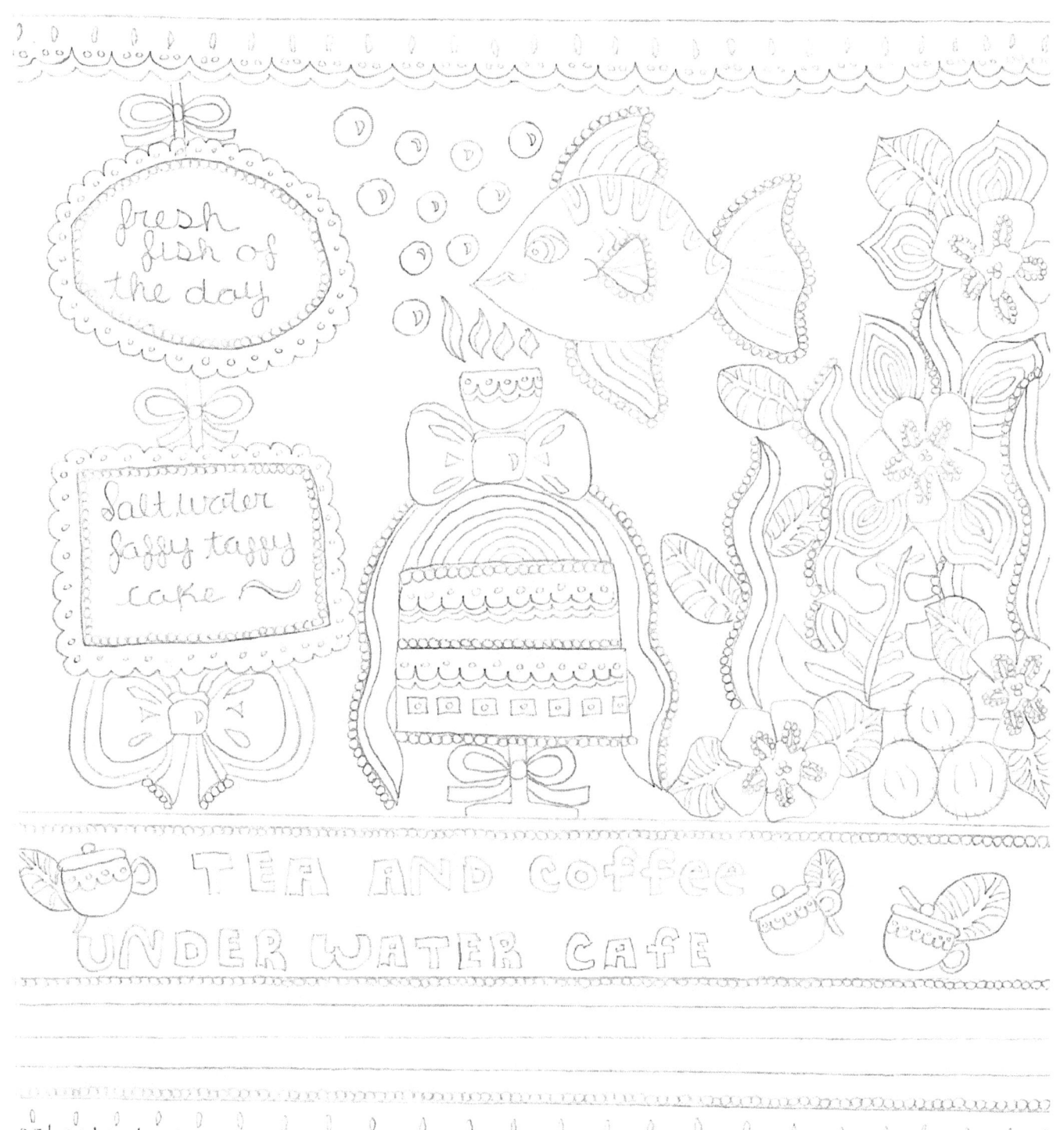

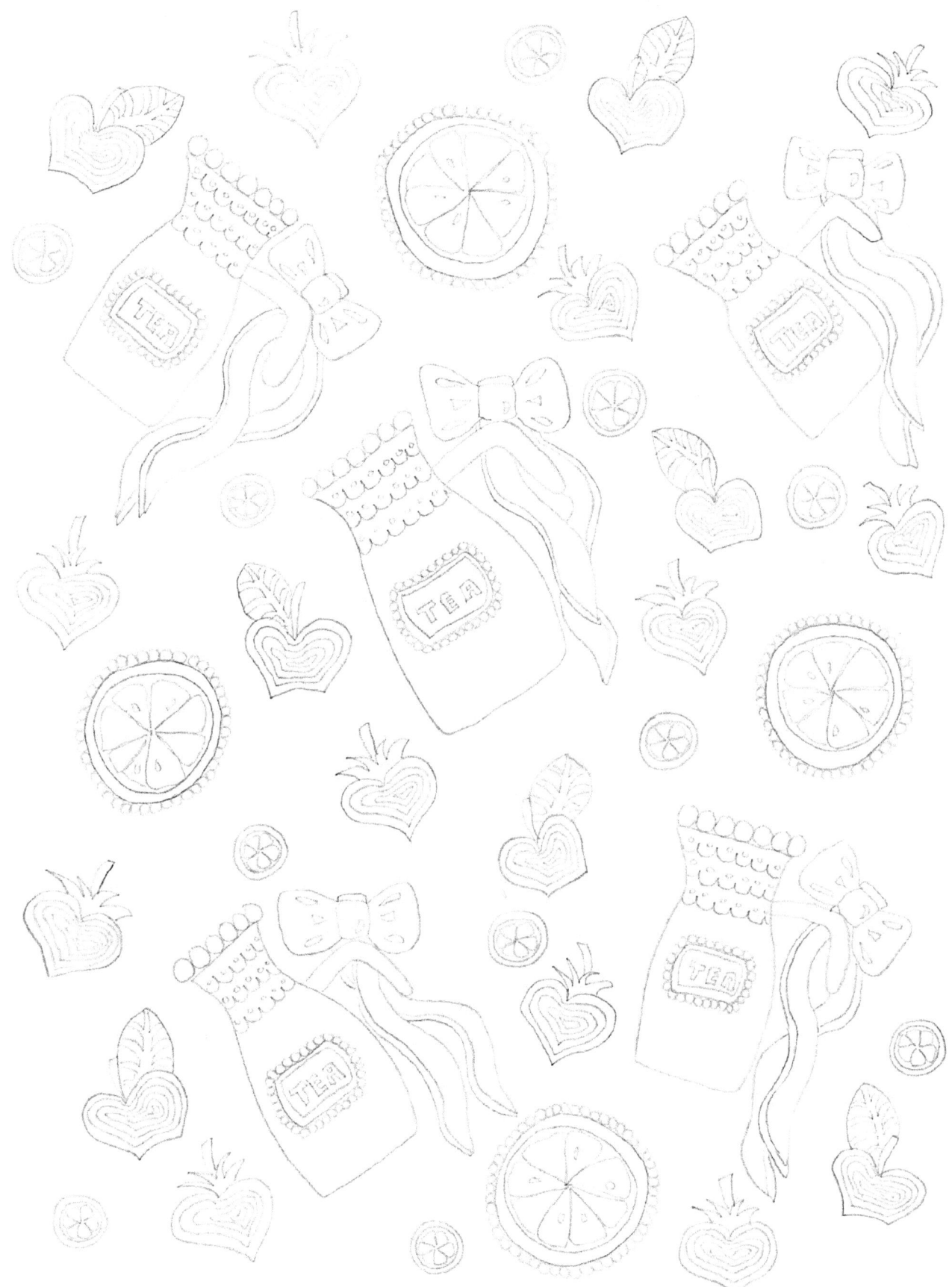

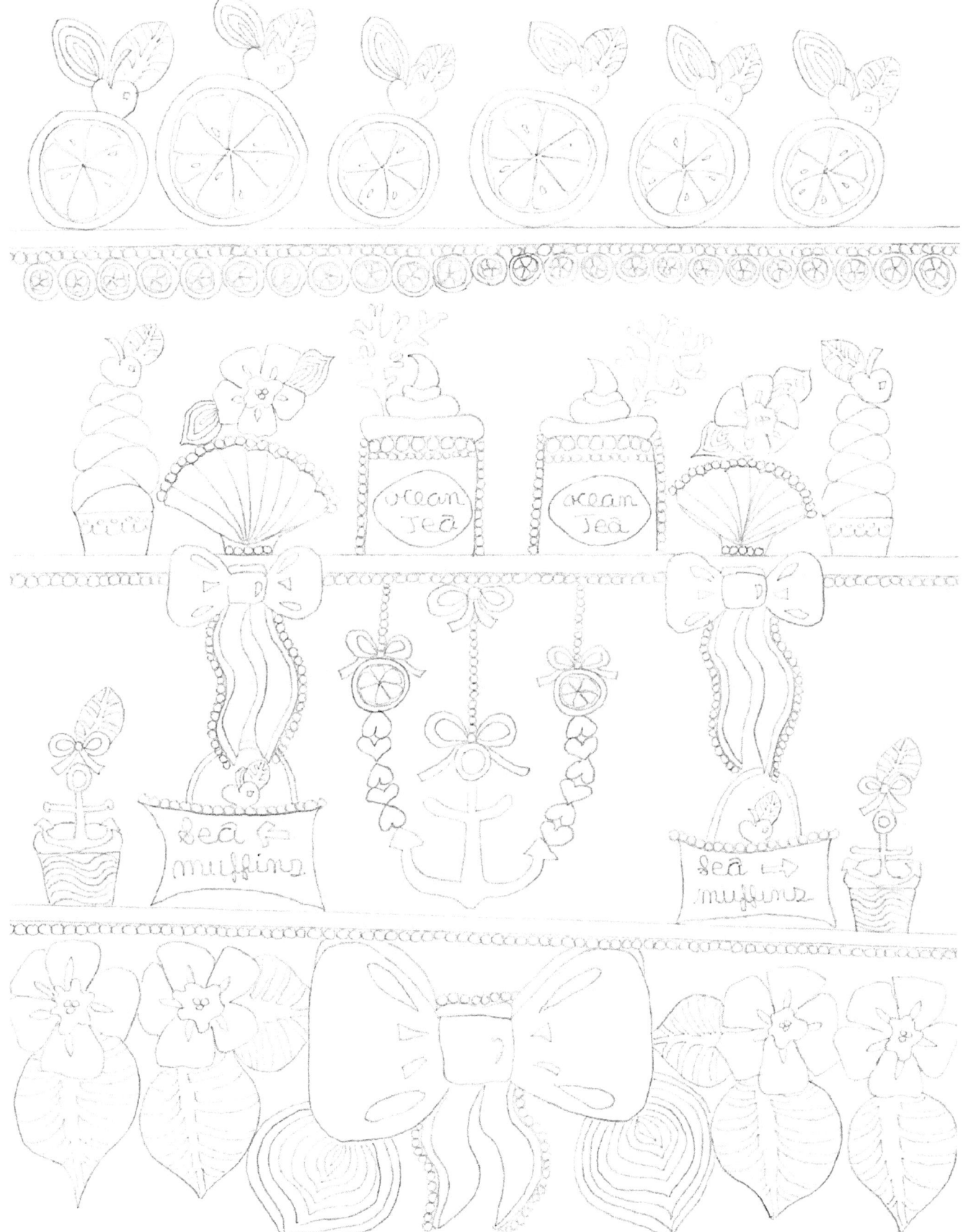

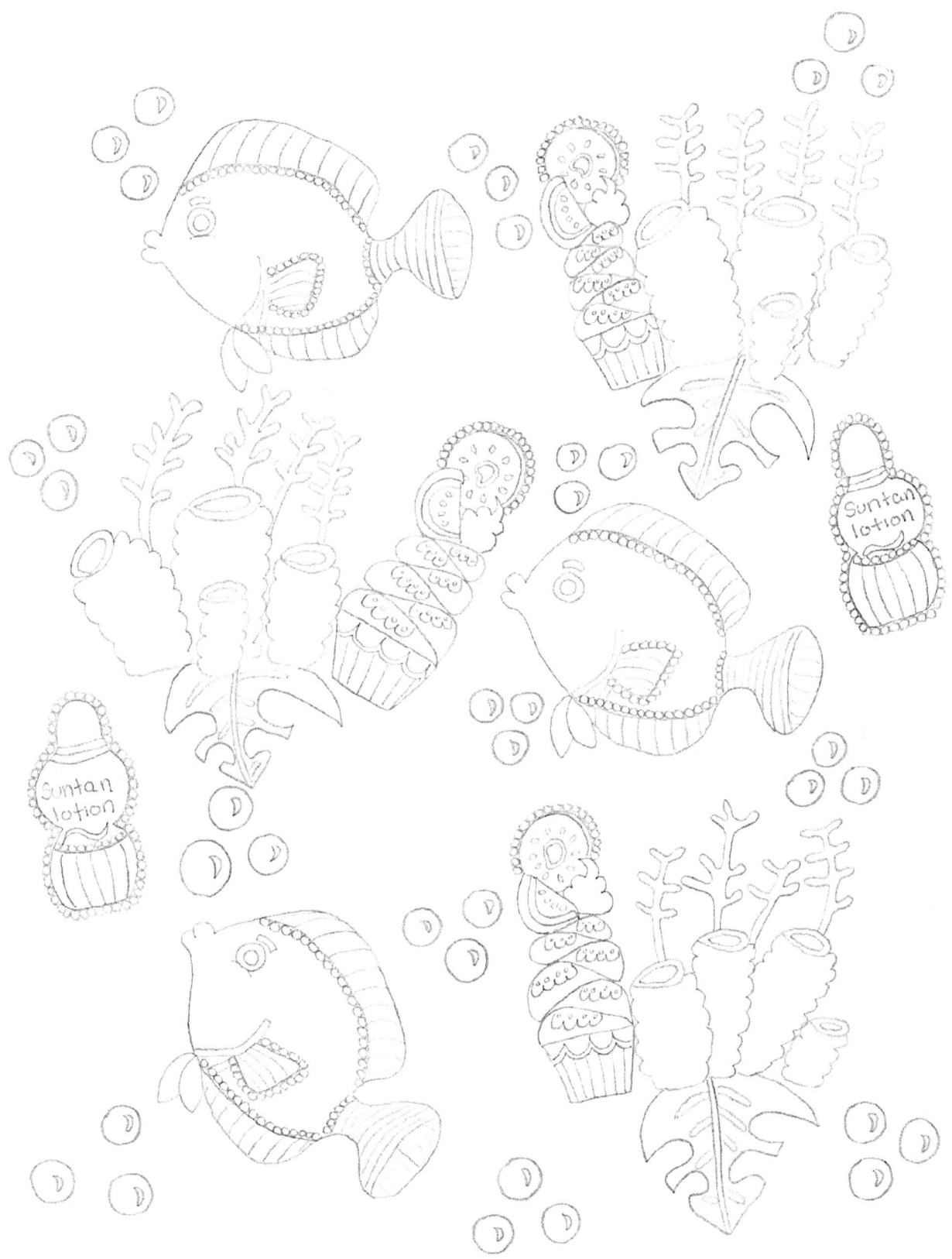

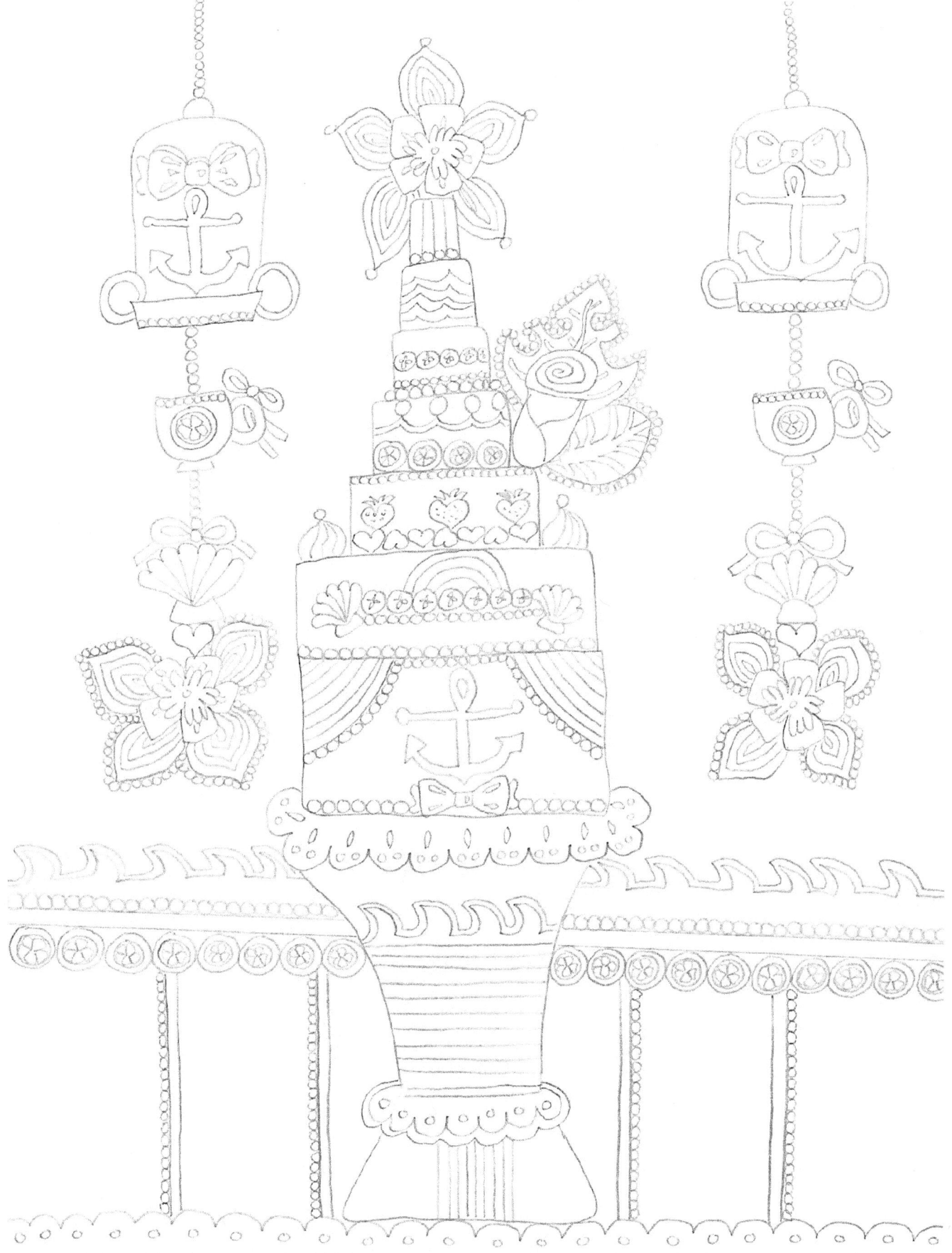

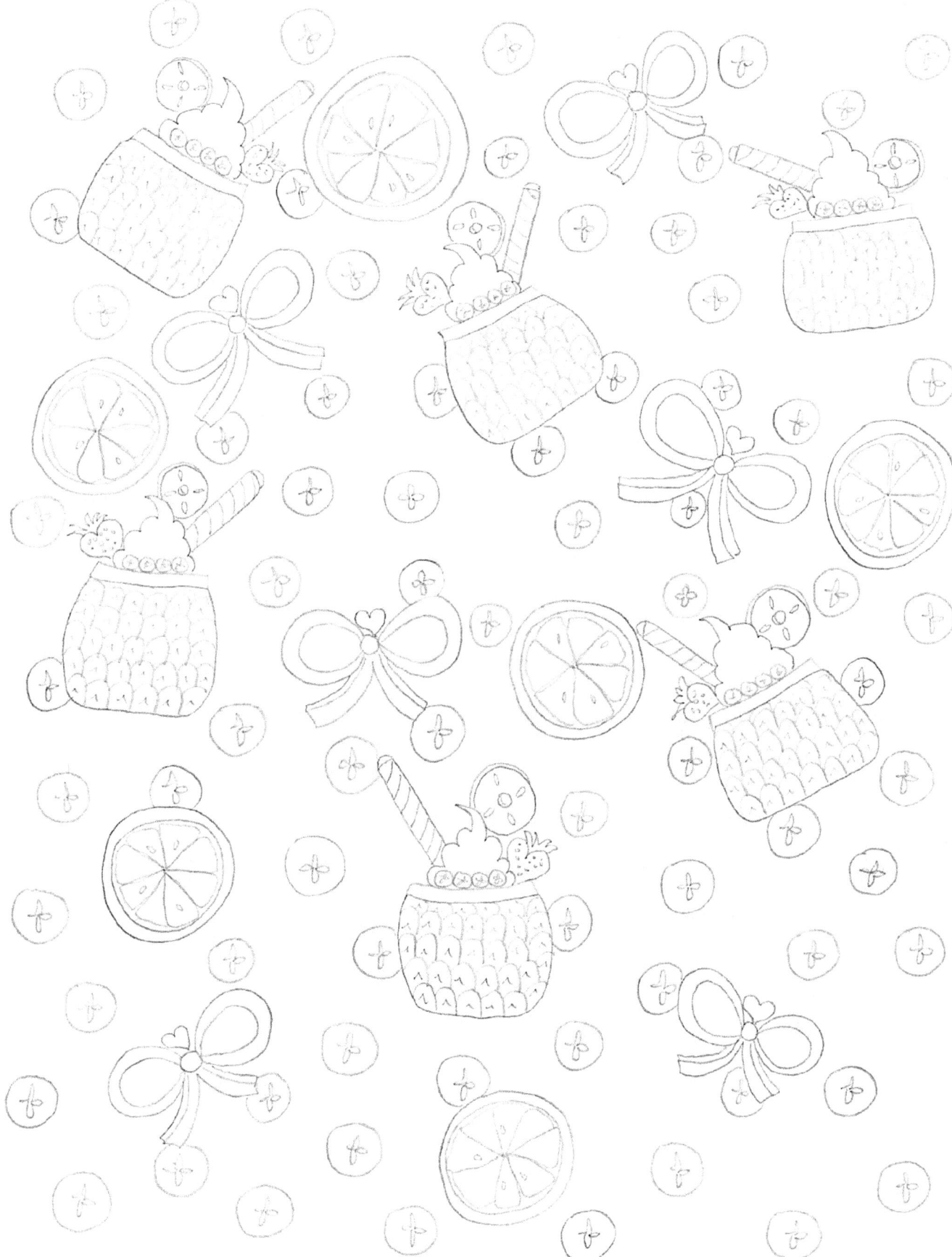

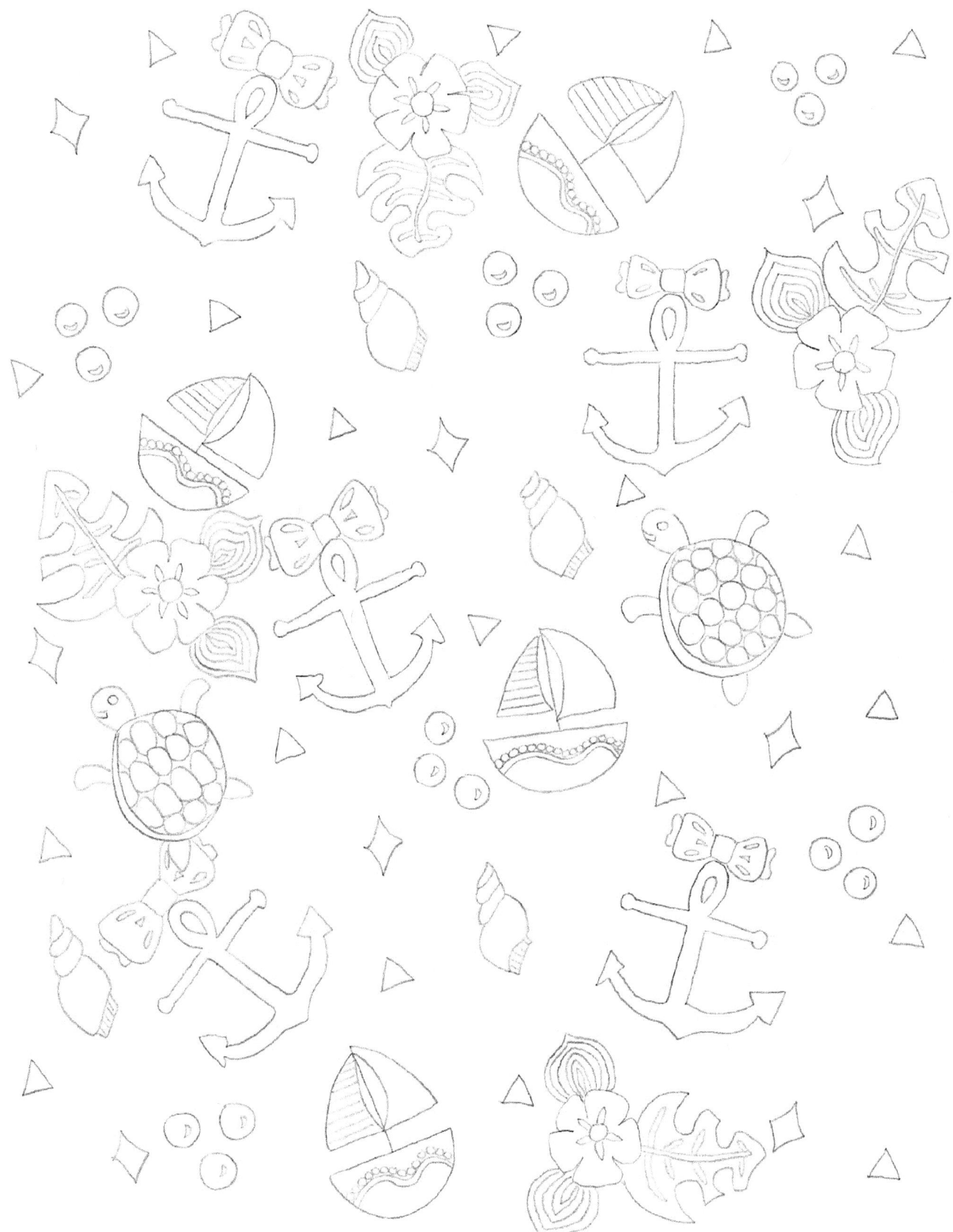

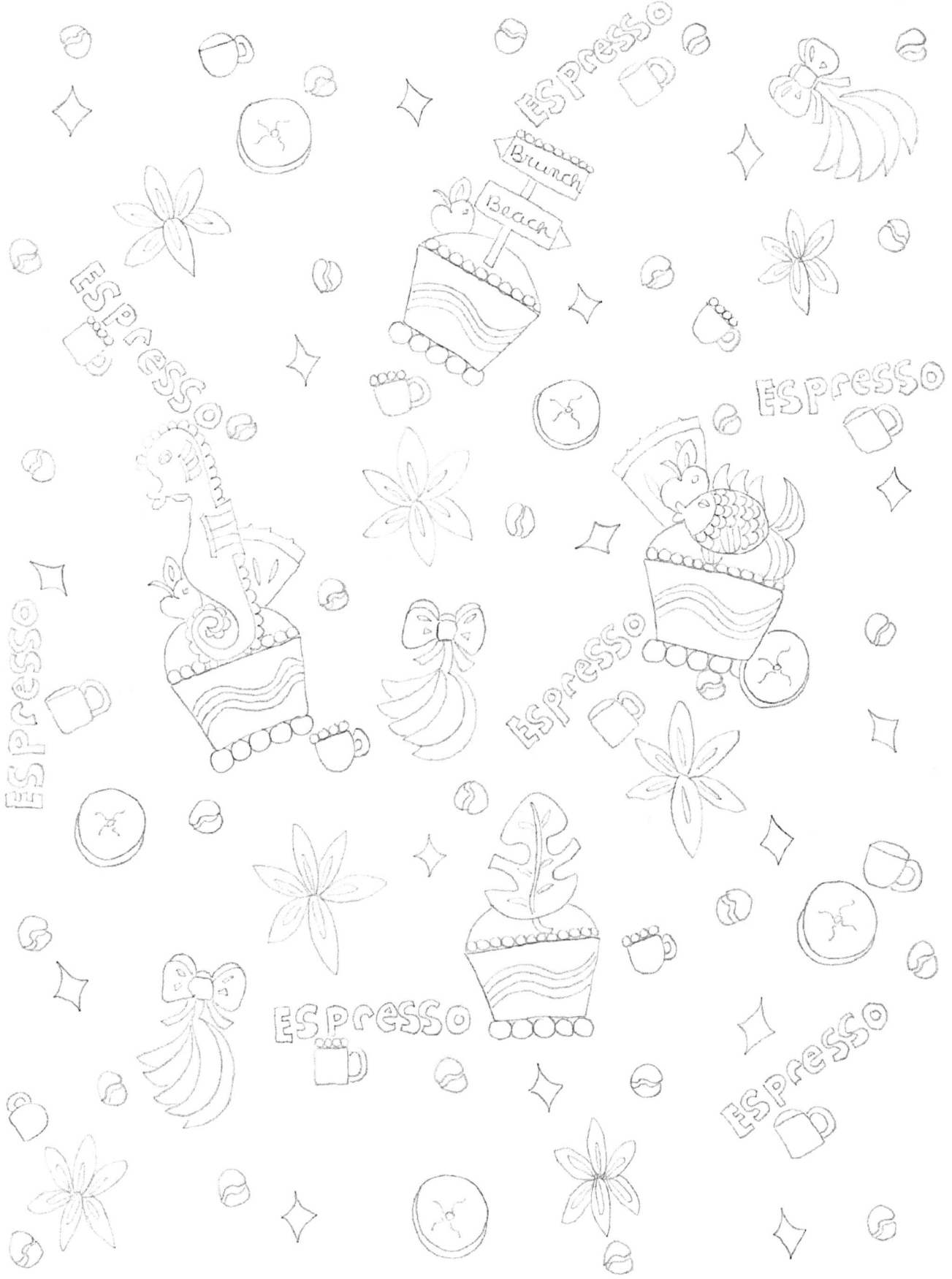

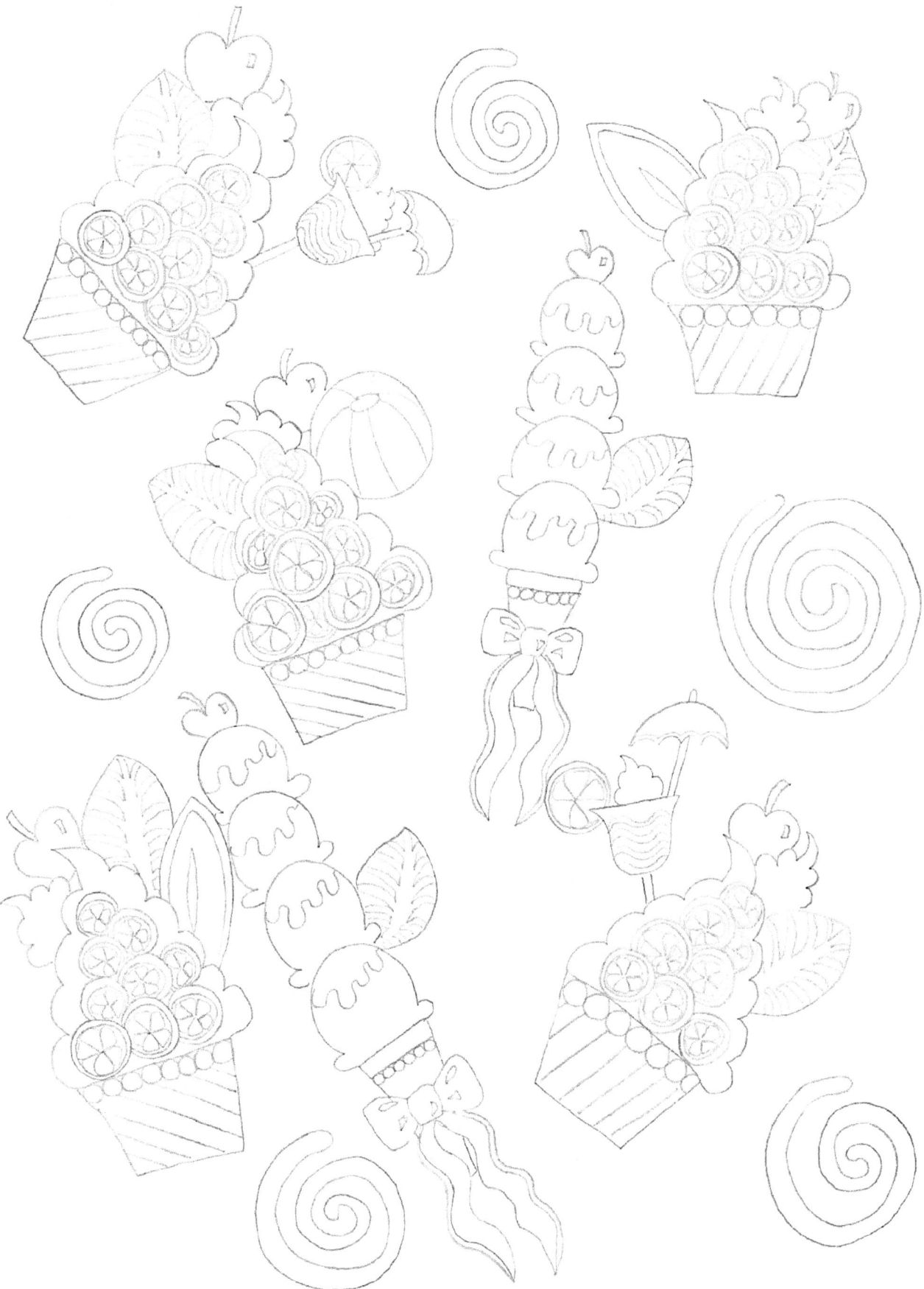

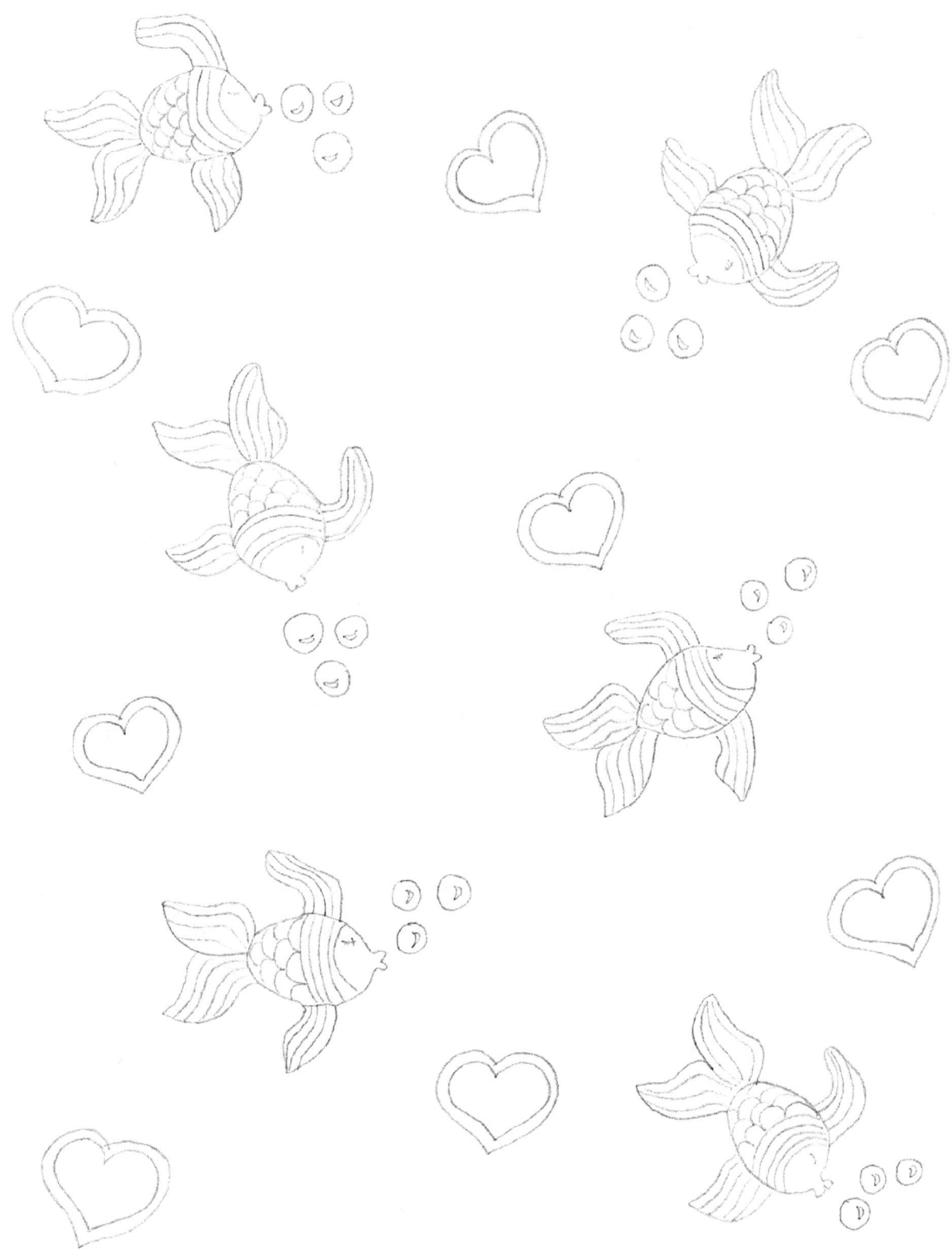

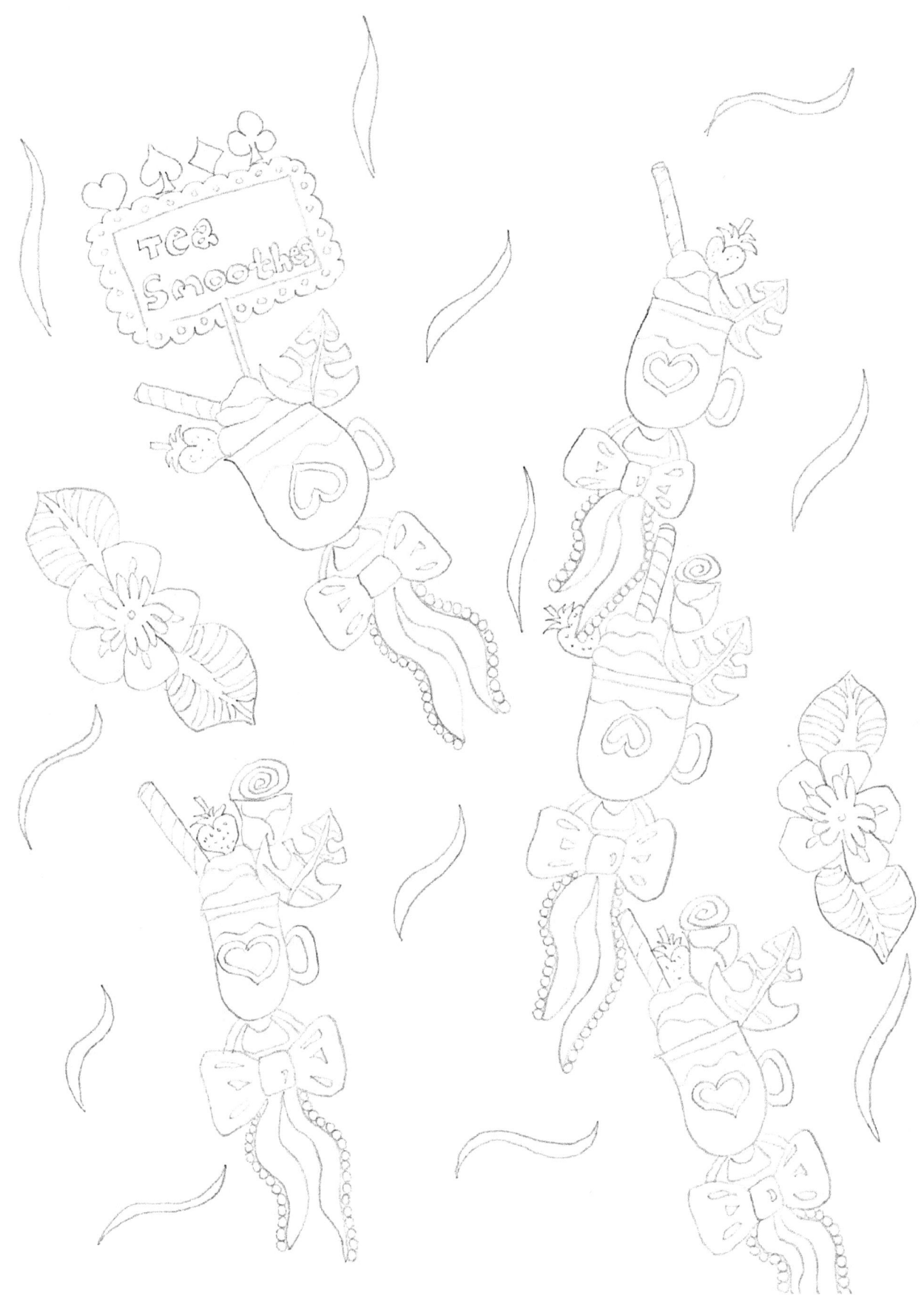

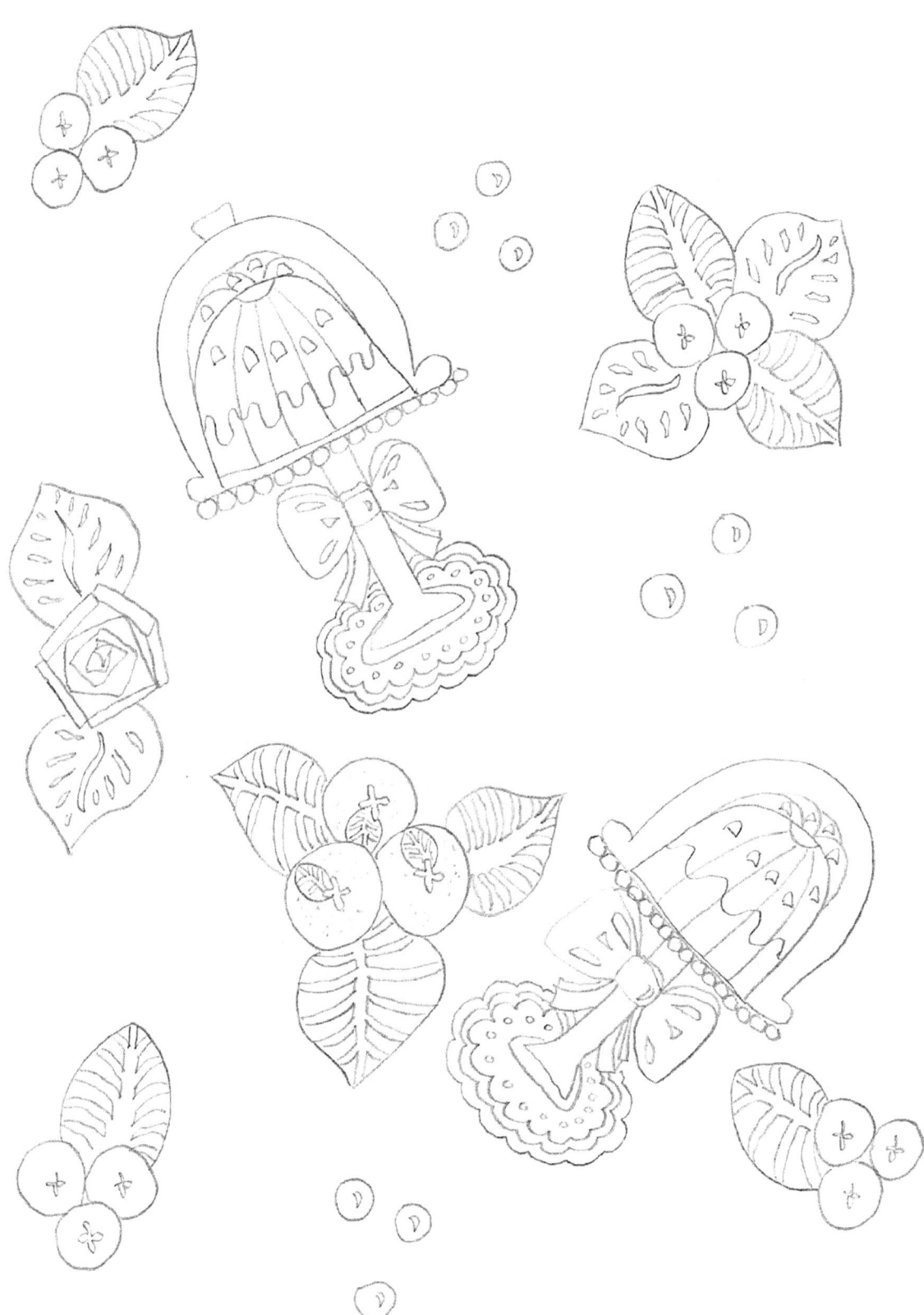

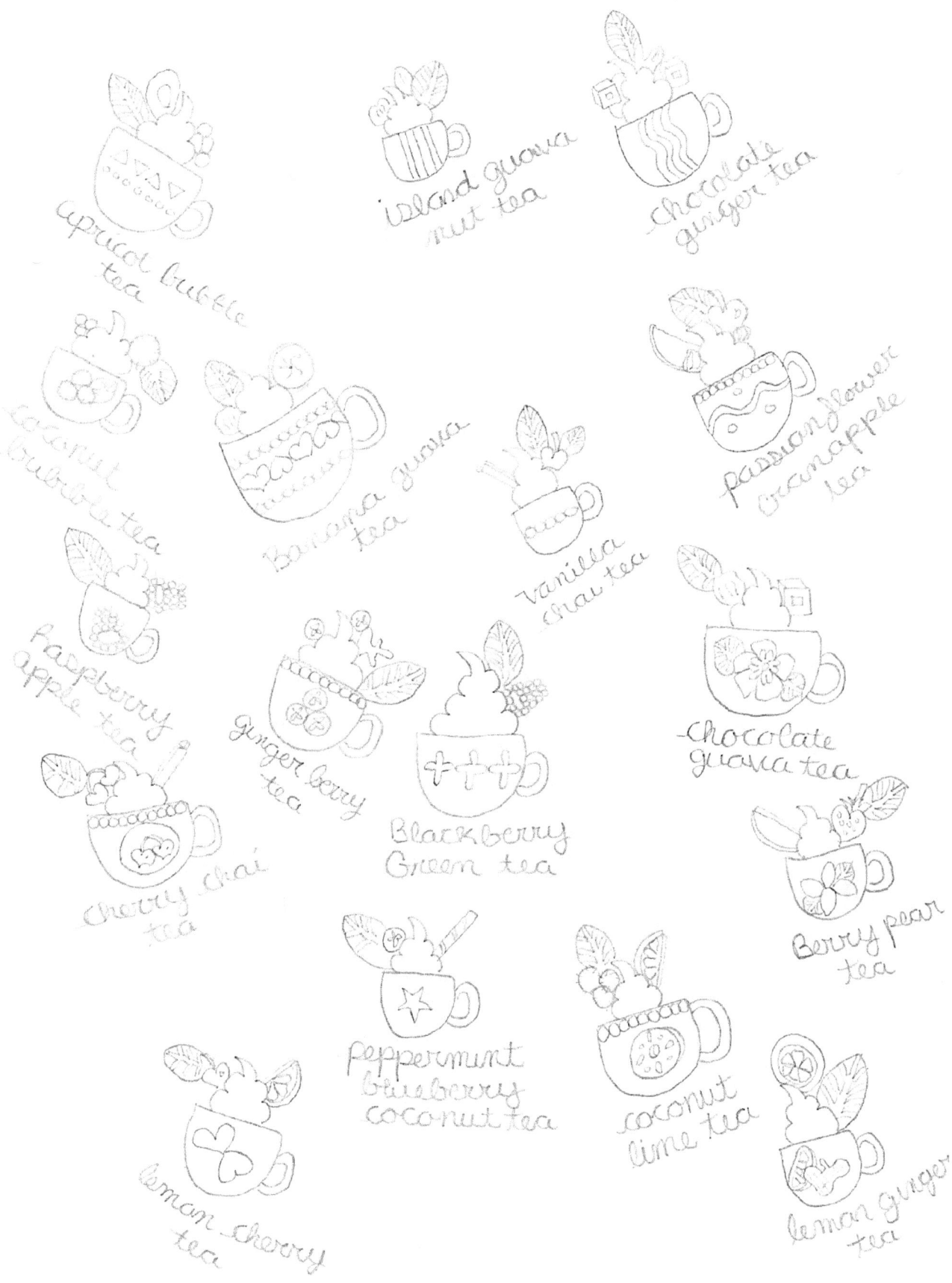

apricot bubble
tea

island guava
nut tea

chocolate
ginger tea

coconut
bubble tea

Banana guava
tea

vanilla
chai tea

passionflower
pineapple
tea

Raspberry
apple tea

ginger berry
tea

Blackberry
Green tea

chocolate
guava tea

cherry chai
tea

Peppermint
blueberry
coconut tea

coconut
lime tea

Berry pear
tea

lemon cherry
tea

lemon ginger
tea

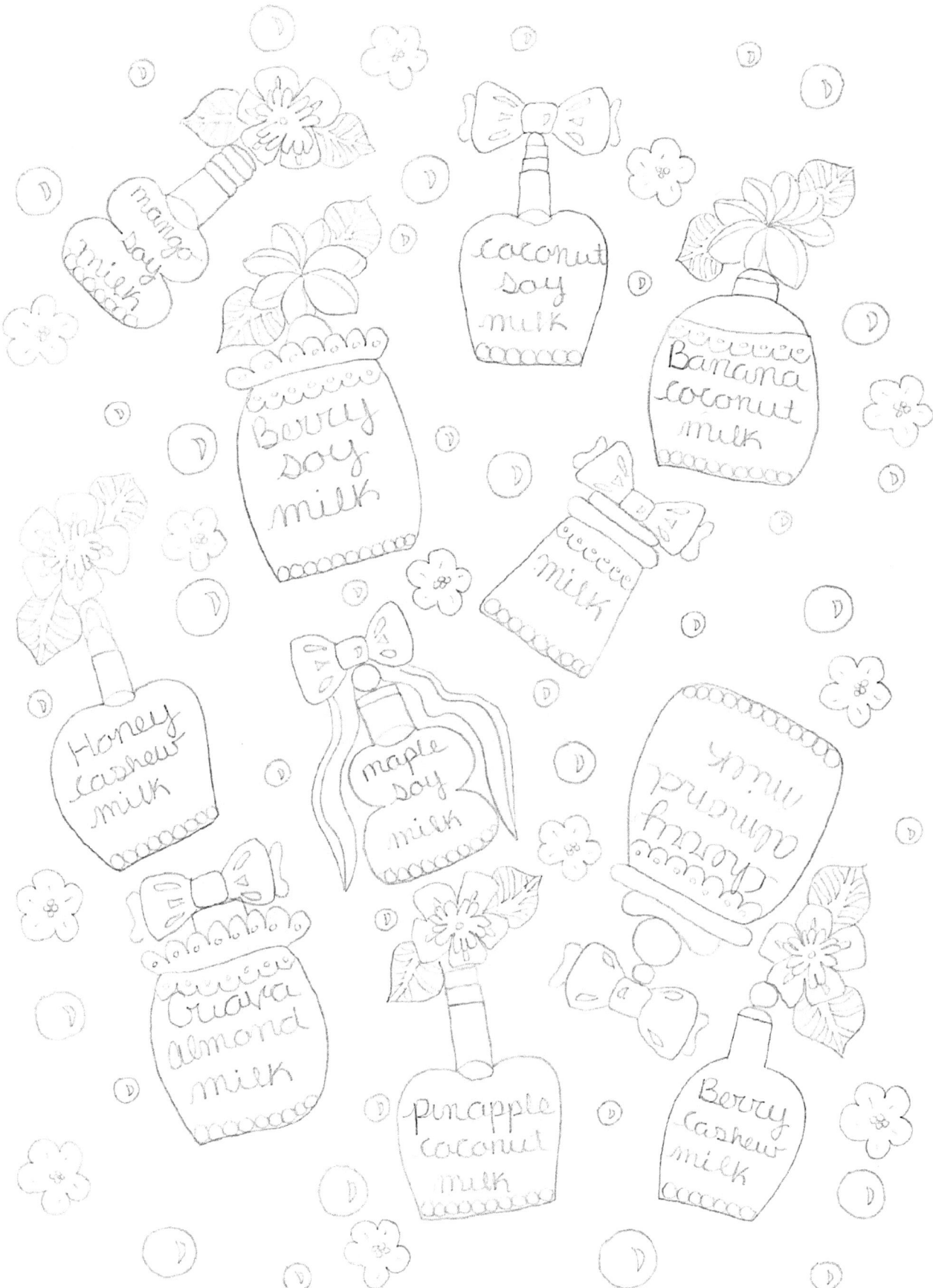

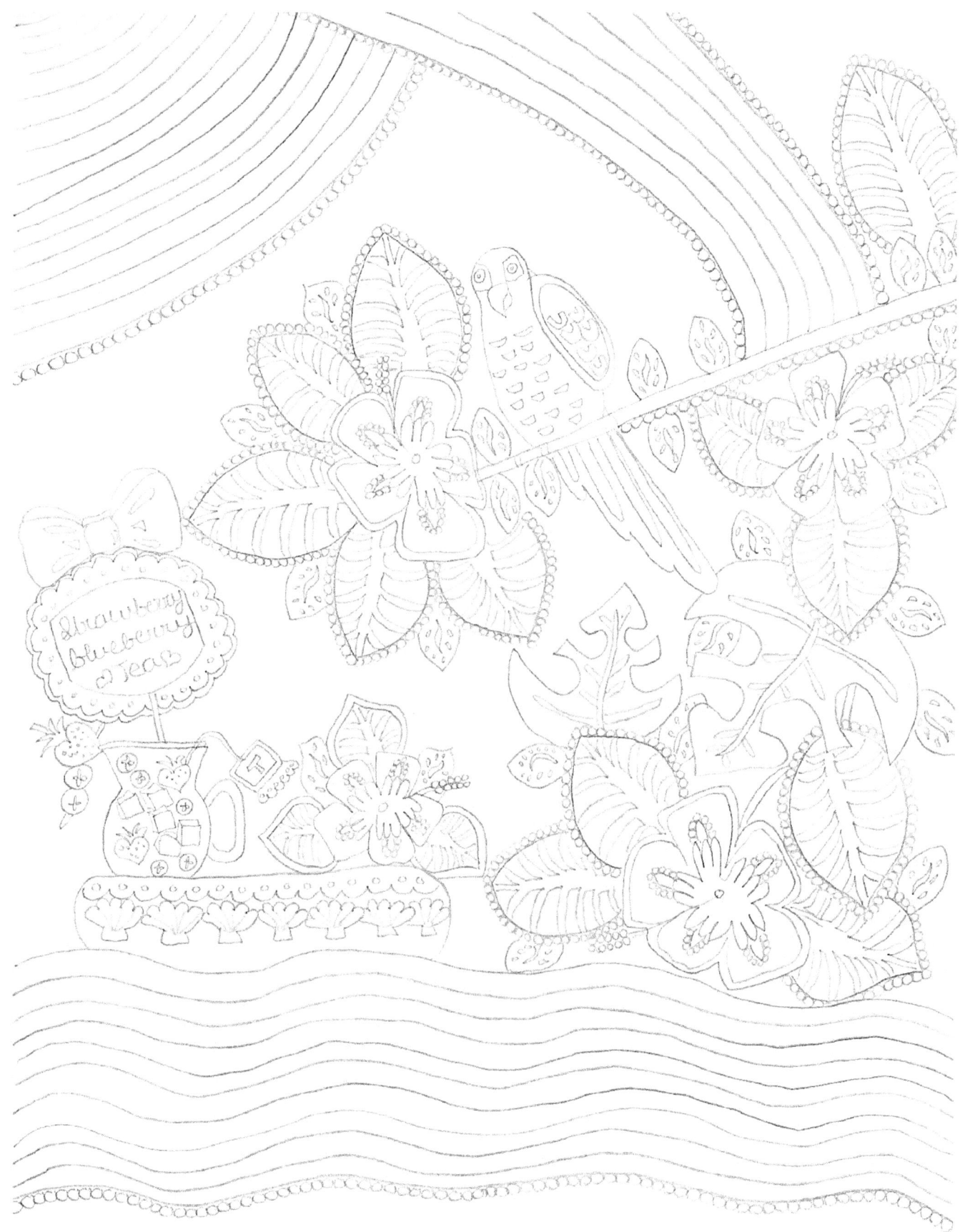

Strawberry
Blueberry
Teas